FRENCHIE'S SOUPS
A Cookbook

by Frenchie Renard
with Alex McCall

FOREWARD

When I put on the first neo-burlesque show in Denver in 1998, I never expected it to become what it is today- a wide variety of shows happening in Denver, and all along the front range of Colorado. This book is filled with a terrific representation of what the current Denver burlesque scene has to offer, and many of these performers are dear to my heart as well as a part of my personal burlesque history.

Kitty Crimson and Fanny Fitztightlee performed in some of my early shows, I had to sneak an underage Midnite Martini into her first performance venues, Cora Vette and I produced shows together and many of the lovely ladies featured on these pages have been students of mine, including the lovely Frenchie Renard, who took her ecdysiast education and ran with it, starting her own show at Voodoo Comedy Playhouse and giving her community another home for their craft.

 Like soup, burlesque is a simmering art form. The opera gloves sliding off, the saucy, come-hither looks are like the first scents of a soup coming together- you know they're going to lead to something delicious. Every soup is at base, a meal in a bowl, but the ingredients and the way they're cooked and spiced and balanced make it special. Burlesque is at base a performer, on the stage, removing clothing, but any fan of the art form knows that every act is special because of what the dancer puts into it. So, to me the pairing is just perfect.

Browse the recipes, gaze at the loveliness pictured inside this book and you'll never look at soup the same again.

Michelle M. Baldwin

"Vivienne VaVoom"

http://www.viviennevavoom.com

http://twitter.com/VivienneVaVoom

"Do you have a kinder, more adaptable friend in the food world than soup? Who soothes you when you are ill? Who refuses to leave you when you are impoverished and stretches its resources to give a hearty sustenance and cheer? Who warms you in the winter and cools you in the summer? Yet who also is capable of doing honor to your richest table and impressing your most demanding guests?

Soup does its loyal best, no matter what undignified conditions are imposed upon it. You don't catch steak hanging around when you're poor and sick, do you?"

Judith Martin ('Miss Manners')

Welcome

In every corner of the world, throughout our history, where people have gathered to eat, there has been soup. Within this book are the recipes of my family and friends, cherished by them, and given to you with love. I hope that you will find your favorite soup between these covers, perhaps a variation on a trusty tried-and-tested recipe known to you already, or perchance a new one to add to your growing repertoire.

About the book… and about me

I'm a home cook and a mother of five based in Denver, Colorado. I'm also a burlesque performer, compere and producer.

Backstage at the inimitable Cora Vette's show one night, a good friend and performer by the name of Eve Harmony watched me drinking from a generous overpour of Irish whiskey and said, "What's that? Frenchie Soup?" And thus, a meme, an in-joke and a catchphrase for the burlesque stage was spawned.

My special recipe for Frenchie Soup is not in this book, but Eve's joke did made me think of the wildly popular soups I took to potlucks and dinner parties, and restorative broths taken to ailing friends and family. It made me think, too, about the skill of matching the right soup to the right person. It's a thing with me. Perhaps it's a thing with you as well?

At its least, this book is just the ultimate spin-off from an in-joke. But it's also the result of dedicated curation of recipes, fund-raising by friends, photo-shoots and plenty of tasting sessions. It's a distillation of recipes from the collections of friends and family, my own collection of stained, frayed, blurry notes and magazine clippings, plus ideas from cookbooks and, inevitably, searches on the internet. It's been a personal activity and a collective one too, lasting over two years and involving many people. I hope all these efforts shine through to you in the final tasting.

INGREDIENTS

Please forgive me a couple of notes on ingredients. Fresh, high-quality ingredients really are the best. Locally-sourced, whole, organic foods make all the difference, where you can find them. Toxins, allergens and artificial chemicals have no business in soup. And nothing beats freshly-ground pepper or freshly-crushed garlic.

Whenever possible, use those fresh ingredients. The difference in taste is remarkable and they're almost always more nutritious than canned or frozen produce. Avoiding canned vegetables is best, due to growing concern among nutritionists about toxins leaching from cans into their contents, particularly tomatoes. Soaking beans overnight is not a big deal and they're both cheaper and lighter to carry back from the shop if they're not canned. Sometimes it takes more effort and sometimes it's more expensive but it's surely worth the effort to try. After all, soup is special and deserves the best!

Some of my recipes require slightly more unusual ingredients, which might also be a spur to support the cultural groceries, food marts and farmers markets of your neighborhood. I love listening to people who know food, about the subtle differences between bacon and pancetta, or whether a Sonora pepper might be better for my soup than a jalapeno.

A suggested soup pantry follows this introduction.

Secret ingredients

Alterations to the recipes are enthusiastically encouraged. That's a beauty of soup, you can tinker with it based on your taste buds and the ingredients on hand in your kitchen, and come up with something marvelous. Soup-making is sometimes improved by a glass of wine, a beer or an occasional "Frenchie Soup". Have fun.

Photos of bowls of soup are difficult to make interesting. So for you, I'm showcasing images of soup alongside a selection of the glamorous and gorgeous performers from Denver's Burlesque, Cabaret, and Variety entertainment scene, set at lovely Denver landmarks. You're welcome!

Continuing the celebration of lovely Denver, my friend and fellow aspiring chef, Ryan Hodros, who is also the resident beer expert at *303 magazine* and *5280 magazine*, provides recommendations on Colorado craft beers and ciders to perfectly accompany the making and service of each of these soups. Cheers!

Equipment

For the most part, all that's required is a clean cutting board, a sharp knife, a wooden spoon, and a sturdy soup pot. A few of the recipes call for specific tools, such as an immersion blender or wok. It's entirely possible to do without these, but they're relatively inexpensive given their usefulness and easy to find in department stores or cookery shops. For example, a regular blender or food processor works perfectly well instead of an immersion blender, but then you'd miss out on the thrill of using a proper power tool in the kitchen, and any fine mesh strainer will work but a chinois is a thing of beauty when it comes to purées.

Health

Some of you may be looking for calorie counters or nutritional information for these soups; you won't find them in this book, on purpose. My philosophy is that everyone's body tells them what they need, so follow your head and your stomach in equal measure. Ingredient swaps are often possible in my recipes, leading to lower calorie or fat content.

A few recipes are decadent by design and just don't work as well without their rich ingredients; Lobster Bisque is a good example of "a little of what you fancy" -- have it rarely but use good butter and heavy cream because it's damn well worth it!

Gluten-free and vegetarian variations are noted, where applicable, and there's also a raw vegan soup (that's unbelievably good).

THANK YOU

I must thank the team of recipe testers employed in the making of this soup cookbook, without whom I can scarcely imagine moving forward with this idea. These recipes have been tested and improved by professional cooks, home cooks, and people who've never made soup without a can opener affording for the best and easiest to follow directions for absolutely anyone who picks up this book and decides to give it a whirl.

Much thanks and a generous overpour of love, to my recipe testers:

> Azure Born, Lucy Britches, Gigi D'Lovely, Neil Dreger, Chakra T. Ease, Aspen Fire Faire, Bunny Galore, Kia Goutte, Jaymie Largent, Gerry Lo, Rhi Long, Stacy D. Luxe, Tara Levin Mack, Terri Mazel-Emet Smolensky, Sapphire Stone, Sarah Taggart, and Rebecca Fitzpatrick Talley.

The hardest working photographer in the business, Mark Palmer, took most of the photos. He is AWESOME and I'm incredibly grateful to share this experience with him. Along for the ride are fellow shutterbugs Dave Sansonne and Anthony Graham, you'll find their professional biographies and contact information at the end of this book.

The Burlesque community at large has been a huge source of support for this cookbook and I am grateful to all. In thanks, I will dedicate a significant portion of proceeds from sales to the Burlesque Hall of Fame Museum and the Legends of Burlesque.

AND FINALLY, A FEW WORDS ABOUT BURLESQUE

Since gleefully entering showbiz a few years ago, I have the opportunity to meet and learn from some of the most amazing people within the world of burlesque and my experiences as a performer, producer and giddy fan afforded me life-affirming, gorgeous, glamorous, and entertaining experiences. I am indeed very lucky to be part of a community of artists celebrating sensuality in all its wonder and variation. And brilliant comedy, always comedy.

Life is short and requires glitter. And soup.

Featured soup pin-ups, and beloved friends of mine:

> Cora Vette, Vivienne Vavoom, Pierre Jean Pierre, Sofia Soubrette, Midnite Martini, Kitty Crimson, Fanny Fitztightlee, Surlie J. Temple, Gigi D'Lovely, Eve Harmony, Sapphire Stone, Chakra T. Ease, Fuchsia LaFae, Neil Down, LaLoux, Chaz Boudoir, Eldryn Phoenix, Mona Del Rio, Carmen Ghia, Deidre Von Derriere, Adam Goldstein, Stacy D. Luxe, Penny Spectacular, Cherry Pop Pop Poppins, plus lovely non-burlesque performers Teri Mazel-Emet Smolensky, Rhi Long, and Sarah Taggart

This book is dedicated to my children; Sarah, Charlotte, Sophie, CJ, and Ruby, soup-lovers extraordinaire and the loves of my life.

xoxo Frenchie Renard

SOUP PANTRY

The List

This is by no means an all-encompassing list, I've listed out some items you'll look for again and again when making soup. They're good things to keep on hand and worth purchasing the best when you can. Keeping these suggested ingredients (and tools) on hand means less last-minute trips to the store!

In Your Cupboards

<u>Dried or Tetra-Pak Beans and Legumes:</u> Cannellini, Navy, Black, Great Northern, Lentils

Pasta: Ditalini, Wide Egg Noodles

<u>Jarred or Tetra-Pak Vegetables:</u> Olives, Tomatoes

<u>Dried Spices:</u> Moroccan Spice Blend, Mexican spices mix, Herbes de Provence, Bay Leaves, Variety of Salts and Peppers

<u>Fresh Spices/Aromatics:</u> Flat-Leaf Parsley, Cilantro, Oregano, Tarragon, Rosemary, Garlic, Onions, Shallots

<u>Oils, Vinegars and Sauces:</u> Good olive oil, Coconut oil, vegetable oil, Balsamic vinegar, Apple Cider Vinegar, Red Wine Vinegar, Cooking Sherry, White wine for cooking, Harissa paste, Hot Sauce, Honey, Maple Syrup, Agave syrup, Peanut Butter

<u>Dried Fruit and Nuts:</u> Sun-dried Tomatoes, Pine Nuts, Walnuts, Raisins, Dates

<u>Grains:</u> Bread Crumbs/Panko, Flour, brown sugar, white sugar, confectioner's sugar

Beef Broth, Chicken Broth, Vegetable Broth

In Your Refrigerator

<u>Vegetables:</u> organic celery, carrots, greens (spinach, collard, kale, etc.), and mushrooms, salad

<u>Dairy:</u> organic heavy cream, organic milk, organic eggs, organic butter, organic sour cream, organic cheeses

<u>Meat:</u> nitrate-free, uncured bacon, pancetta, sausages, fresh or roasted chicken, Mason Jar with bacon drippings, Soup stock/broth

<u>Condiments:</u> Mayonnaise, Mustards, Jams and Spreads

<u>Fruit:</u> lemons, limes

In Your Freezer

Frozen fruit and vegetables, especially peas, spinach, and berries

Beef bones, ham hocks, sausages

Soup stock

On Your Counter

Apples, Squash, Potatoes, Onions, Seasonal fruit

Tools

Keep at least one good chef's knife and keep it sharp, along with at least two cutting boards: a plastic one for vegetables, glass or plastic for cutting meat and seafood, a wooden one for chopping veg. This helps tremendously in preventing cross-contamination. [More on food safety in a bit] Invest in a great stockpot, a saute pan, a fry pan, a grill pan, and saucepan. Keep wooden spoons, spatulas, and tongs near your stove.

Whether you are on a tight budget or just dislike clutter, keeping a kitchen full of fresh ingredients, with few pre-prepared and heavily processed items is quite freeing. You know where all your food comes from and how it was prepared. And it is so simple to feed yourself from your own kitchen!

Shopping

Aim for organic, fresh ingredients, and for animal products to be locally-sourced, responsibly-raised, free of fillers, artificial chemicals, or antibiotics.

For those occasions when you can't soak beans or get fresh ingredients, more producers are offering beans and tomatoes, broths and soup in lovely, recyclable Tetra-Paks these days, which pleases me much!

Dried herbs only last a few months after opening, so I tend to buy the smallest jar or bag I can find, or look for the small packets of fresh versions that pop up in the produce department of every store I'm in — just enough cilantro, or fresh basil, and so on, to keep and use for a few days.

My dream is to have a kitchen garden but someone else will have to tend to it, I have the opposite of a green thumb. A shame, really, a kitchen herb garden looks smart and is so very handy.

Check out the counters at your favorite grocer's or specialty grocers. I invariably will pick up shredded rotisserie chicken and already prepared (cleaned, chopped) vegetables when I'm there for nights I'm rushed or not feeling up to fussy prep work, and having the butcher or seafood clerk do the heavy lifting is something I cannot resist. Cleaning crabs at home is just nonsense, for example.

FOOD SAFETY

For the health and well-being of your family and guests, it is vitally important you follow some basic food safety rules when cooking, most of which are of the common sense variety. Wear protective gloves when handling raw meat or seafood. Wash your hands thoroughly and often. Store food properly (at the right temperature, for the right amount of time) and cook meat and seafood to a safe temperature.

STOCKS

Stocks are easily found in grocery stores and relatively inexpensive – I frequently use them when I am pressed for time – but I do encourage you to make your own when you can. A really good broth can stand on its own, and all you need is a big sturdy pot, bones (it's important you blanch the bones separately to remove impurities before adding to the stock pot) and vegetables/spices. Vegetable broth is even easier – it can be made richer with vegetarian bouillon, and there is a product called "Not Chick'n" bouillon that, when added to vegetable broth, does a cracking job of mimicking chicken broth and strengthens the stock.

DO NOT SALT YOUR STOCK. By the time it's boiled and simmered for several hours, any salt you add will make the broth overly salty and potentially ruin your eventual soup. Instead, add a couple of bay leaves, some other fresh herbs, and fresh peppercorns.

Bring everything to a strong boil for ten minutes or so, then reduce to a simmer for several hours for bone broth and about an hour for vegetable broth. Use a fine-mesh strainer to pull all the vegetables, spices, and bits of meat from the broth. Store broth in a plastic container with a tight-fitting lid.

With stock and soup, if you aren't immediately going to use or serve it, it needs to be properly cooled, i.e. an ice bath in the sink, brought down to nearly room temperature before being refrigerated. Bacteria love warm, moist things, so don't let your soup cool all the way to room temperature on the stove and ruin all your good work.

Properly cooled and stored, stock lasts for months in your freezer. Every time I roast a chicken or turkey I reserve the bones for stock, and if I remember to ask, I'll get marrow bones or ham bones from the butcher at the grocery store and throw them in my freezer, too. Whenever you cut carrots, celery, onion…save those ends and greens for your next stock!

RECIPES

Chapter: From Around the World

"Only the pure in heart can make a good soup."

Ludwig van Beethoven

Frenchie Renard, at
Denver's City Park

FRENCHIE ONION

My first soup, *naturellement*, is French Onion.

Way back in school, on the occasion of my first school dance, my date thought it would be wonderful to take me and our double-date friends to a local French restaurant. Stymied by the bilingual menu, the others looked to me to sort out what they should eat. First up: *Soupe d'oignon.*

Faced with this incredibly aromatic crock of bubbling cheese, they said, in anxious unison, "What is this and how do we eat it?"

Fellow onion soup lovers know you just dive in. The decadent melted Gruyere; the crisp wheel of a baguette slice, the mysterious dark depths of the fragrant broth; the slippery onions...the earliest printed recipe for this sop, or bouillon, was produced in the early 1600's -- what you see here is not much changed from that.

One of the easiest, most inexpensive, and best satisfying recipes in this entire cookbook, I challenge you to begin your soup-making odyssey with this recipe for authentic French Onion Soup.

If you, like me, are overly-sensitive to onion fumes, I recommend wearing a pair of swimming goggles for this preparation - it really works.

DIFFICULTY LEVEL:
- Easy

INGREDIENTS:
- 6 large onions (about 5 lbs.), sliced thinly
- 1/2 stick (1/4 cup) unsalted butter
- 1 tbs all-purpose flour
- 1 1/2 quarts beef broth
- 12 thick slices (½") of baguette, toasted
- 3/4 pound coarsely grated Gruyère cheese

DIRECTIONS:
- In a large kettle cook the onions in the butter over medium heat, stirring frequently, for 40 minutes, or until golden brown.
- Sprinkle the onions with the flour and cook the mixture, stirring, for 3 minutes, to make a roux.
- Add the broth slowly, whisking constantly until it comes to a boil, and simmer, covered, for 20 minutes. Season with salt and pepper.
- Put 2 slices of the toast in each of 6 heated soup bowls, top each toast with 1 tablespoon of the Gruyère, and pour the soup over the toasts. Further fanciness suggests broiling the toast and cheese for 3 minutes before adding to the soup, and by all means, yes, serve in a darling little crock.

VARIATIONS:
- Gluten-free: use gluten-free flour and choose a gluten-free baguette
- Vegetarian/Vegan: substitute vegetable broth enriched with bouillon for beef, Olive or Coconut oil for butter, and use vegan cheese

RYAN RECOMMENDS:
"A classic soup deserves a classic brew, and there's nothing more classic in Colorado than New Belgium's Fat Tire Amber Ale. The toasty notes compliment the crouton in your Frenchie Onion soup, and the smoothness and low ABV (alcohol by volume) means you can have a few without ruining your meal."

EldRyn Phoenix, at Denver's
Botanic Gardens

PHOENIX COLCANNON

"If it was raining soup, the Irish would go out with forks."

Brendan Behan

From the Emerald Isle, a comforting potato, leek, and kale concoction held dear by those with Guinness and/or whiskey hangovers, from County Cork to Corpus Christi.

I substitute bacon grease for the butter, but you can use olive oil, coconut oil, vegetable oil, shortening – or whatever type of fat pleases you. The smoky flavor imbued by the bacon just makes me very happy!

DIFFICULTY LEVEL:

- Easy

INGREDIENTS:

- 1 tbs butter
- 2 lbs Yukon Gold potatoes, peeled and cut into ½" cubes
- 2 leeks, thinly sliced (white portion only)
- 1 medium yellow onion, chopped
- 3-1/2 cups chicken broth

- 1/4 cup heavy cream
- Salt and pepper, to taste
- 1 bunch kale (5-oz), rinsed, trimmed, and coarsely chopped
- 1 tablespoon olive oil

DIRECTIONS:

- Preheat oven to 375.
- Heat the butter in a medium saucepan over medium heat. Add leeks, onion, and 1/4 teaspoon salt; cook 3 minutes or until tender (do not brown). Add potatoes and broth; bring to a boil. Cover, reduce heat, and simmer 15 minutes or until potato is tender.
- If you like your soup chunky, stop here and allow soup to cool. Prepare the kale as noted and add the cream to cooled soup, then reheat and top with roasted kale.

- For a smooth soup, use an immersion blender to purée the soup (or transfer the soup to a food processor or blender and purée in batches). When cooled, strain with a chinois (or other fine mesh strainer), stir in cream, and salt and pepper (to taste). Reheat.
- Toss kale with oil, salt and pepper. Spread kale on a rimmed baking sheet and bake for 10 to 15 minutes or until kale is crispy and slightly browned on the edges, stirring every 5 minutes.
- Ladle soup into 6 bowls; garnish evenly with roasted kale.

VARIATIONS:

VEGETARIAN: substitute vegetable broth for chicken; vegetable oil for butter; coconut cream for heavy cream

RYAN RECOMMENDS:

"Between the butter and bacon and the heavy cream, you're going to need some crisp, bitter flavor to cut the richness and clear your palate. Dale's Pale Ale by Oskar Blues Brewing is well-blanced, nicely bitter, and great paired with this smoky soup."

Fuschia LaFae, at Denver's Cheesman Park

FAE MULLIGATAWNY

From the United Kingdom, by way of India, is the wildly delicious Mulligatawny. If you've never had this famous Anglo-Indian fusion food, you're in for a treat!

Seinfeld fans should remember Mulligatawny from "The Soup Nazi" episode. You enjoyed the gags, now eat the soup.

DIFFICULTY LEVEL:
- Moderate

INGREDIENTS:
- 9 tbsp. unsalted butter
- I tsp. Aleppo pepper
- ½ tsp. cumin seeds
- ½ tsp. coriander seeds
- ½ tsp. black mustard seeds
- 2 dried chiles de arbol
- I plum tomato, minced
- 3 tbsp. minced ginger
- 6 cloves garlic, minced
- I large yellow onion, minced
- ½ jalapeño, minced

- ¼ cup flour
- I tbsp. ground coriander
- 2 tsp. ground cumin
- I½ tsp. ground turmeric
- 9 cups chicken stock or vegetable stock
- I¾ cups red lentils
- 3 tbsp. minced cilantro
- I cup canned coconut milk
- ¼ fresh lemon juice
- Kosher salt and freshly ground black pepper, to taste
- Plain yogurt, to garnish

DIRECTIONS:
- Cook 5 tbsp. butter, Aleppo, cumin, coriander, mustard, chiles, and tomato in an 8" skillet over high heat until fragrant (be sure not to burn!); set sauce aside.
- Heat remaining butter in a 6-qt. saucepan over medium-high heat. Add ginger, garlic, onion, and jalapeño; cook until browned, 15 minutes. Add flour, coriander, cumin, and turmeric; cook until smooth, 2 minutes. Add stock and lentils; boil. Reduce heat to medium-low; cook, covered, until tender, 45 minutes. Add cilantro; purée. Add coconut milk, juice, salt, and pepper; divide among bowls. Garnish with sauce and yogurt.

VARIATIONS:
- Vegetarian: substitute vegetable oil for butter; use soy yogurt

RYAN RECOMMENDS:
"It might seem obvious to pair an Indian-inspired soup with an India Pale Ale, but once you've tried Hop Haze IPA from J Wells Brewery, you'll be all-aboard this idea. With big hops flavor and a sour twist, this will more than stand-up to the spicy flavors of this soup."

Mona del Rio, at Denver's Sloans Lake

BLACK MAGIC BEAN

Here in the Western U.S. where I live, we truly love our Mexican friends and are deeply grateful for their bounty of delicious food. This black-bean soup is made New Mexico-style, but you won't care where it comes from once you've tried it.

DIFFICULTY LEVEL:
- Easy

INGREDIENTS:
- 28 oz. black beans, along with their soaking "juice"
- I cup chopped pancetta (or 8 bacon slices chopped)
- I small onion, cut into 1/4-inch dice (3/4 cup)
- 1/2 red bell pepper, cut into 1/4-inch dice (3/4 cup)
- I 1/2 teaspoons chopped garlic
- 1/2 teaspoon finely chopped and seeded fresh jalapeno chile
- I 1/2 teaspoons dried oregano, crumbled
- I bay leaf
- 1/2 teaspoon dried thyme, crumbled
- 2 quarts chicken broth
- 3/4 teaspoon white pepper
- 2 tablespoons chopped fresh cilantro
- Accompaniments: sour cream and chopped fresh cilantro

DIRECTIONS:
- Cook bacon in a 5- to 6-quart heavy pot over moderately high heat, stirring occasionally, until golden, about 5 minutes.
- Transfer bacon with a slotted spoon to a small bowl and pour off all but I tablespoon fat from pot.
- Reserve 2 tbs chopped bacon for topping, return remaining bacon to pot and heat over moderately high heat until hot -- but not smoking.
- Add onion, bell pepper, garlic, chile, oregano, bay leaf, and thyme and sauté, stirring frequently, until onion is softened (about 5 minutes).
- Add beans, chicken broth, and pepper and simmer, partially covered, stirring occasionally, until beans are very tender (about 2 1/2 hours).
- Discard bay leaf and stir in cilantro.
- Serve soup topped with sour cream, chopped cilantro, and reserved bacon. Have some warmed tortillas, or tortilla chips, handy: you'll want to sop up every drop.

VARIATIONS:
- Vegetarian: eliminate pancetta; replace chicken broth with vegetable broth

RYAN RECOMMENDS:

"Ska Brewing's Mexican Logger is the perfect accept to this South-of-the-Border offering. Its light, it's refreshing, and it'll keep you cool as you wait for the beans to cook."

Carmen Ghia, at Casa Bonita

REVVED TORTILLA SOUP

My friends in Denver often choose tortilla soup when making soup from scratch and there's little wonder why: it's easy and inexpensive to make and pays off with incredible flavor.

Diced Hatch green chiles, grown in the Hatch Valley of New Mexico, make ALL the difference.

DIFFICULTY LEVEL:
- Easy

INGREDIENTS:
- 2 teaspoons olive oil
- 1 medium-sized onion, chopped
- 4 garlic cloves, minced
- 1 medium-sized jalapeno pepper, chopped
- 4 oz. diced green chile peppers (Hatch green chiles if you can get them)
- 1/2 medium red pepper, chopped
- 4 small bone-in chicken breasts
- 1/2 cup dry white wine
- 2 teaspoons cumin
- 1 teaspoon chili powder
- 1/4 teaspoon cayenne pepper
- 56 oz. chicken broth
- 28 oz. diced tomatoes
- 16 oz. red enchilada sauce
- 1 cup tortilla chips (garnish/topping)
- 1 tbs. sour cream
- ½ cup shredded cheddar cheese

DIRECTIONS:
- Sauté onion, garlic, jalapeño and green chile peppers with olive oil in a large pot until softened.
- Add all the rest of the ingredients to the large pot and bring to a boil. Cook 15 minutes at a rolling boil.
- Remove the chicken breasts and shred. I find it's easiest to shred with a fork and a knife (time saver: at the deli counter at your grocery store they'll often have shredded rotisserie chicken ready to go!)
- Return shredded chicken to the pot and simmer an additional 45 minutes.
- Serve, topped with chopped avocado, a drizzle of sour cream, a dusting of shredded cheddar cheese and crushed tortilla chips for dazzling effect.

VARIATIONS:
- Use an immersion blender to transform into a decadently smooth soup, topping with a bit of shredded chicken along with the avocado and chips.
- Vegetarian: substitute tofu or seitan for chicken; vegetable broth for chicken; vegan cheese and sour cream (or omit them all together).

RYAN RECOMMENDS:
"Sometimes pairing like flavors is fun, so why not try Bootstrap Brewing's Backfire Chili Ale with this chili-laden soup? This beer tastes strongly of BBQ potato chips (not a bad thing!) and leaves you refreshed, not overwhelmed with heavy flavor – perfect for a soup that walks on the spicy side."

Deirdre von Derriere,
Chez Frenchie

PASTA FA-DROOL, A.K.A. PASTA E FAGIOLI

Buon Giorno, Italia! I hope you'll forgive me, but I've had to leave traditional Italian wedding soup out of this book, because I couldn't decide which of the many recipes I was given was the best. Too much cursing, yelling and throwing of plates!

DIFFICULTY LEVEL:

- Easy

INGREDIENTS:

- 3 tablespoons of olive oil
- 2 large garlic cloves, minced
- I large carrot, finely chopped
- 2 celery, finely chopped
- I small onion, finely chopped
- I/3 cup finely chopped pancetta or bacon
- 6 peeled, seeded and chopped ripe roma tomatoes

- I quart chicken broth
- 28 oz. cannellini beans
- I I/4 cup small pasta (Tubetti or Ditalini)
- I/3 cup chopped fresh parsley
- Salt and pepper
- Dash Of red pepper flakes
- Shaved parmesan cheese

DIRECTIONS:

- Heat the garlic in the oil in a large heavy pot, just until you catch the aroma. Remove garlic and chop. Cook the onion, carrot, pancetta, and celery until soft.
- Add the chopped garlic and cook another minute. Pour in the broth, beans and chopped tomatoes, and cook for I5 minutes.

- Remove a few scoops of the bean mixture and puree or mash, then return to the pot.
- Add the pasta, chopped parsley and seasonings.
- Cook until the pasta is cooked *al dente*.
- Serve in bowls topped with a drizzle of olive oil, the shaved cheese and a sprinkling of chopped parsley.

VARIATIONS:

- Gluten Free: use a gluten-free pasta
- Vegetarian: eliminate bacon/pancetta and substitute vegetable broth and vegan cheese

RYAN RECOMMENDS:

"A smooth Italian soup pairs very nicely with a smooth, flull-flavored lager, and you can't go wrong with my personal favorite, Upslope's Lager. It's refreshing, crisp, and just hoppy enough to compete with the bigger flavors of this soup."

Naughty Pierre and Sofia Soubrette,
at Lannie's Clocktower Cabaret

HOT SOUBRETTE AND NAUGHTY SOUR SOUP

Oh sure, you've ordered hot and sour soup at Chinese restaurants and take-out. Maybe you've been to Chinatown and thought the soup you ate there was legit. This, my friends, is THE hot and sour soup.

Getting the ingredients for this soup requires a trip to an Asian market, which always fills me with glee. So much to see and smell. Remember to stock up on a big bag of rice, Chinese beer, Japanese sodas and spicy rice crackers while you're there!

DIFFICULTY LEVEL:
- Very challenging

INGREDIENTS:
- 5 ounces boneless pork loin, cut into 1/4-inch-thick strips (2/3 cup)
- 2 teaspoons dark soy sauce
- 4 small Chinese dried black mushrooms
- 12 small dried tree ear mushrooms
- 1 1/2 tablespoons cornstarch
- 12 dried lily buds (sometimes called golden needles)
- 1/2 cup canned sliced bamboo shoots, cut lengthwise into 1/8-inch-wide strips
- 2 tablespoons red wine vinegar
- 2 tablespoons rice vinegar (not seasoned)
- 1 tablespoon light soy sauce
- 1 1/2 teaspoons sugar
- 1 teaspoon kosher salt
- 2 tablespoons peanut oil
- 4 cups reduced-sodium chicken broth
- 3 to 4 oz firm tofu (about a quarter of a block), rinsed and drained, then cut into 1/4-inch-thick strips
- 2 large eggs
- 2 teaspoons Asian sesame oil
- 1 1/2 teaspoons freshly ground white pepper
- 2 tablespoons thinly sliced scallion greens
- 2 tablespoons fresh whole cilantro leaves

DIRECTIONS:
- Toss pork with dark soy sauce in a bowl until pork is well coated.
- Soak black and tree ear mushrooms in 3 cups boiling-hot water in another bowl (water should cover mushrooms), turning over black mushrooms occasionally, until softened, about 30 minutes. (Tree ears will expand significantly.) Cut out and discard stems from black mushrooms, then squeeze excess liquid from caps into bowl and thinly slice caps. Remove tree ears from bowl, reserving liquid, and trim off any hard nubs. If large, cut tree ears into bite-size pieces.
- Stir together 1/4 cup mushroom-soaking liquid (discard remainder) with cornstarch in a small bowl and set aside.
- Meanwhile, soak lily buds in about 1 cup warm water until softened, about 20 minutes, then drain. Trim off tough tips of lily buds. Cut lily buds in half crosswise, then tear each half lengthwise into 2 or 3 shreds.
- Cover bamboo shoots with cold water by 2 inches in a small saucepan, then bring just to a boil (to remove bitterness) and drain in a sieve.

- Stir together vinegars, light soy sauce, sugar, and salt in another small bowl.

- Heat a wok over high heat until a bead of water vaporizes within 1 to 2 seconds of contact.

- Pour peanut oil down side of wok, then swirl oil, tilting wok to coat sides.

- Add pork and stir-fry until meat just changes color, about 1 minute, then add black mushrooms, tree ears, lily buds, and bamboo shoots and stir-fry 1 minute.

- Add broth and bring to a boil, then add tofu. Return to a boil and add vinegar mixture. Stir

- cornstarch mixture, then add to broth and return to a boil, stirring as the liquid thickens. Reduce heat to moderate and simmer 1 minute.

- Beat eggs with a fork and add a few drops of sesame oil. Add eggs to soup in a thin stream, stirring slowly in one direction with a spoon.

- Stir in white pepper, then drizzle in remaining sesame oil and divide among 6 to 8 bowls.

- Sprinkle with scallions and cilantro before serving.

VARIATIONS:

- Vegetarian: substitute tofu for pork loin; eliminate eggs, swap veggie broth for chicken broth.

RYAN RECOMMENDS:

"Flavor-wise, I'm inclined to pair this Asian-inspired soup with Yak and Yeti's Chai Milk Stout but if it's ambiance you're after, try Lucky Drink Co.'s Lucky Buddha Enlightened Beer. The beer's not that great to be honest, but the Buddha shaped bottles are the coolest-looking glassware around."

Adam Goldstein near
the Blue Bear at the
Denver Convention Center

TROUBADOUR MINESTRONE

I could swear I've never had the same Minestrone twice in my life, even in my own kitchen. The basics are usually the same: beans, veg, pasta, tomatoes. But, oh, the variations!

Italian mamas and grannies will tell you: *"mangia la minestra o salta dalla finestra!"* Loosely translated as, "eat this minestrone or jump out the window, *stupido.*"

DIFFICULTY LEVEL:
- Easy

INGREDIENTS:
- 2 quarts broth (beef or vegetable)
- 1/2 cup dried cannellini or a cup of fresh beans.
- 1 packed cup each: shredded spinach, kale, and cabbage
- 1 clove of garlic, crushed
- Fresh parsley
- Mirepoix: minced carrot, celery and onion
- 1 zucchini, diced
- 1 potato, diced
- 28 oz. plum tomatoes
- 1/2 cup rice
- Salt and pepper to taste
- Boiling water
- Grated parmesan cheese

DIRECTION:
- If the beans are dried, soak them overnight.
- Heat the shredded greens in a soup pot just until they wilt and drain well.
- Add remaining vegetables and simmer in the broth. When they're almost done (when you taste a piece of potato and find it is soft but not falling apart), season, add the rice, and continue cooking, stirring gently. The rice should serve to absorb excess liquid, but if the soup gets too thick, add some boiling water.
- Serve the soup with the grated cheese and accompany with some gorgeous, warm Italian bread.

RYAN RECOMMENDS:
"Made right, this is one of the most elegant soups in your repertoire, and demands an elegant brew as accompaniment. I suggest 12 Degree Brewing's Walter's White for its sour notes, medium body, and low ABV (because you aim to keep things classy)."

*Kitty Crimson, at a
classic car show in Denver*

CRIMSON BORSCHT

From the heart and hearth of central and Eastern Europe, comes the bright, bold and wholly comforting borscht. There's controversy about its spelling and its origins but it tastes great nonetheless.

This is a soup that nourishes and enriches your strength and fires your passions -- romantic or otherwise. Making this soup will win you adoration, love, and gifts of vodka. All good things!

DIFFICULTY LEVEL:
*   Moderate

INGREDIENTS:
*   8 cups beef broth
*   I pound slice of meaty bone-in beef shank
*   I large onion, peeled, quartered
*   4 large beets, peeled, chopped
*   4 carrots, peeled, chopped
*   I large russet potato, peeled, cut into 1/2-inch cubes
*   Greens from the beets, washed and roughly chopped
*   2 tbs olive oil
*   3/4 cup chopped fresh dill
*   3 tablespoons red wine vinegar
*   I cup sour cream
*   Salt and pepper to taste

DIRECTIONS:
*   Bring 4 cups of the beef broth, the beef shank, and onion to boil in large pot. Reduce heat, cover, and simmer until meat is tender, about I hour 30 minutes.
*   Transfer meat to work surface; trim fat, sinew and bone and discard. Chop meat; cover and chill. Cool broth slightly. Chill in pot until cold, at least 4 hours and up to I day.
*   Spoon fat from top of chilled broth and discard. Add remaining 4 cups broth, beets, carrots, and potato; bring to boil. Reduce heat, cover, and simmer until vegetables are tender, about 30 minutes.
*   Stir in meat and 1/2 cup dill; cook for about I5 minutes. Season to taste with salt and pepper. Stir in vinegar.
*   Preheat oven to 350. Combine the chopped beet greens with olive oil and salt and pepper. Spread on a shallow baking sheet and roast in the oven for I5 minutes, or when the greens are lightly toasted.
*   One way to enjoy the result is to strain out all the vegetables and have a Borscht consommé. Or you can blend everything with an immersion blender (or blender or food processor) and strain until silky smooth. I prefer my Borscht bold and chunky, so I stop here and eat it.
*   Ladle soup into bowls. Add a handful of roasted beet greens and top with sour cream and remaining dill.

VARIATIONS:
*   Vegetarian: substitute vegetable broth for beef; eliminate beef shank; substitute soy yogurt or coconut milk for the sour cream

RYAN RECOMMENDS:
"Sweet, beefy, and rich in flavor, this Russian soup needs something rather Imperial to stand up with it, and Breckenridge Brewery's Regal Imperial Pilsner fits that bill. Be mindful of that high ABV, lest you fall asleep in your bowl!"

SOUP

RECIPES

Chapter: Chicken

Chicken soup. Whether with noodles, rice, kreplach, chock-a-block with Pho veg or strained into broth, nothing beats chicken soup. It brings comfort, healing, and a sense of everything being right with the world.

"A Jewish woman had two chickens. One got sick, so the woman made chicken soup out of the other one to help the sick one get well."

Henny Youngman

MAZEL MATZOH BALL

Matzoh Ball soup is a sacred thing, to be sure. In a pinch or rush, I've made it from the box (adding a handful of wide egg noodles, carrots and celery to the broth) and no plagues descended on my home. Still, I say you've got to go big or go home: this is the original, old-country bubbe's recipe you'll find at the best Jewish delis.

Don't be afraid of the chicken feet -- they're available from your butcher or specialty food market, and they lend a very specific flavor to this soup that old timers swear by, but you can leave them out if it's not for you without sacrificing a bit of the restorative effect of this soup.

DIFFICULTY LEVEL:
- Challenging

INGREDIENTS:
- 12 sprigs fresh dill
- 4 cloves garlic, thinly sliced
- 3 sprigs fresh cilantro
- 2 small yellow onions, thinly sliced
- 1 bunch celery, cut into 1/2" pieces
- Sprigs from 1/2 bunch flat-leaf parsley plus 1 tbsp., chopped
- 3 large carrots, peeled and cut into 1/2" pieces
- 1 turnip, peeled and cut into 1/2" pieces
- 1 parsley root, cut into 1/2" pieces
- 1 3 1/2-lb. chicken
- 1 lb. chicken feet
- Salt, to taste
- 2 tbsp. seltzer water
- 1/8 tsp. dried dill
- 2 eggs, at room temperature
- 1/2 cup plus 1 tbsp. matzo meal

DIRECTIONS:
- Gather dill, garlic, cilantro, onions, celery, and parsley sprigs in a piece of cheesecloth to form a purse; secure with twine. We'll call this the 'dill purse'.
- Make a second purse with the carrots, turnips, and parsley root. We'll call this the 'carrot purse'.
- Put the dill purse, chicken, chicken feet, salt, and 1 1/2 gallons water into a large pot; bring to a boil. Reduce heat to medium-low; simmer, covered, for 1 1/2 hours. Add the carrot purse and simmer, covered, until carrots are tender, about 30 minutes.
- Remove and discard the dill purse and the feet. Remove the chicken and the carrot purse; let cool. Pull enough breast meat into fine shreds to make 3/4 cup. Reserve 1 cup vegetables from the carrot purse.
- Cover and chill shredded chicken and vegetables. (Reserve remaining chicken and vegetables for another use.) Strain broth through a fine sieve; cool and chill overnight.
- Skim off and discard all but 2 tbsp. chicken fat from broth; set fat aside. Whisk together reserved chicken fat, seltzer, dried dill, and eggs in a bowl. Pour in matzo meal while whisking. Cover and chill the matzo mixture for 15 minutes.
- Bring 2 1/2 quarts salted water to a boil. With wet hands, form matzo mixture into 1" balls. Reduce heat to medium; drop in balls. Cook, covered, for 15 minutes. Stir gently and simmer, covered, until balls are fluffy, 10–12 minutes more.
- Meanwhile, transfer reserved shredded chicken, mixed vegetables, and broth to a large pot; heat over medium heat. Transfer balls to the broth.
- Serve soup garnished with remaining parsley and drink in the accolades.

- Vegetarian: eliminate eggs and chicken feet; substitute vegetable stock, tofu or seitan for chicken.

RYAN RECOMMENDS:

"For this, there can be no doubt: Dry Dock Brewing's Apricot Blonde is your choice. Don't let the fruit notes in this beer fool you, it's the perfect complement to the rich, chicken flavor in this soup — and ups the healthy feeling you'll enjoy."

Eve Harmony, in the studio

EVE'S BOTT BOI, A.K.A. PENNSYLVANIA DUTCH CHICKEN POT PIE

Want to upset me and listen to be rant like an old man on a porch? Try to pass off a frozen tiny pie plate of mechanically-separated chicken pieces and a dank gravy, covered with greasy crust, as "chicken pot pie".

Let's think about this for a moment: would the wonderfully resourceful and healthy Pennsylvania Dutch people choose to give a poor-quality chicken-and-vegetable pie a special name? No, they would not.

Real chicken pot pie is a decadently rich chicken broth with potato, vegetables, and pie pastry dumplings. The pie is not on top of the pot, it is happily bubbling within the pot.

My children were raised on this, as was I, and we'll thank you not to tinker with the recipe as it is perfect already. Foolproof.

DIFFICULTY LEVEL:

- Moderate

INGREDIENTS:
Stock

- Bone-in chicken breasts (2) and thighs (2-3)
- Pinch of saffron threads
- vegetables: carrot, celery, onion, garlic cloves
- Chicken broth

- 3-4 medium potatoes
- Fresh parsley
- Salt and pepper

Dough

- 2 cups all-purpose flour
- ½ tsp salt

- 3-4 tbs vegetable shortening, butter or lard

DIRECTIONS:
Stock

- Cook chicken pieces, saffron threads, and vegetables in 60% water/ 40% chicken broth (more than enough to cover the chicken pieces) in a medium stock pot for 2-3 hours, or until meat is fully cooked.
- Remove chicken pieces and allow them to cool.

- When the chicken pieces are cool, pull meat from bones and reserve chicken meat.
- Discard skin and bones. Remove and discard vegetables.
- Strain the broth. (Stock can be made in advance)

Broth

- Add potatoes and a handful of chopped parsley to broth.
- Season with salt and pepper to taste.

- Bring to a rolling boil and cook until potatoes are tender (15-20 minutes)

Dough

- While the potatoes are cooking, make the dough. NOTE: These dumplings are what make this pot pie, so *don't screw it up:*
- In a bowl, combine flour and salt. Add shortening until mixture is crumbly (resembling pastry crust).
- In a separate bowl, combine egg and milk. Add liquid to flour mixture and combine with a fork to form a soft, yet roll-able dough.
- Place dough on a floured work surface, form it into a disc, and roll to approximately the

thickness of of pie crust. Using a pizza wheel (or, or accurately, a pastry wheel), cut into 2"x 2" squares. Be sure to use plenty of flour to keep the dough from sticking to the surface or the rolling pin, but some flour left on the dough will help to thicken the broth.

- With the broth at a rolling boil, drop dough squares one at a time into the pot, stirring every so often. Maintaining a very gentle boil, cook the dough for 4-6 minutes.
- Add the reserved chicken, more chopped fresh parsley and season with salt and pepper.

In the unlikely event you have leftovers, this chicken pot pie is even better the next day.

VARIATIONS:

- Vegetarian: substitute vegetable stock, tofu or seitan for chicken

RYAN RECOMMENDS:

"A hefty slice of bread should accompany this hearty dish — or even better, Black Shirt Brewing's Pale Red Rye. It's beautifully boozy, with toasty notes and peppery rye that's a lovely complement to this soup."

RECIPES

Chapter: Vegetable

"An old-fashioned vegetable soup, without any enhancement, is a more powerful anti-carcinogen than any known medicine."

James Duke MD (USDA)

Well put, Dr. Duke. Your vital vitamins and minerals, your anti-inflammatory goodness and your all-around health-giving tasty vegetables – all in handy soup form.

If you were to add one of these beauties to your daily menu, I say you could forgo those supplements and maybe take a day off from the gym. Just think of the relief and happiness your internal organs will feel when the goodness of vegetable soup hits 'em. Why, you deserve an extra glass of wine just for making this soup!

Vegetable-based soups are good for what ails ya. Our recipe testers secretly traded these recipes between themselves and hoarded their results in their freezers like chocolate bars or winning lottery tickets.

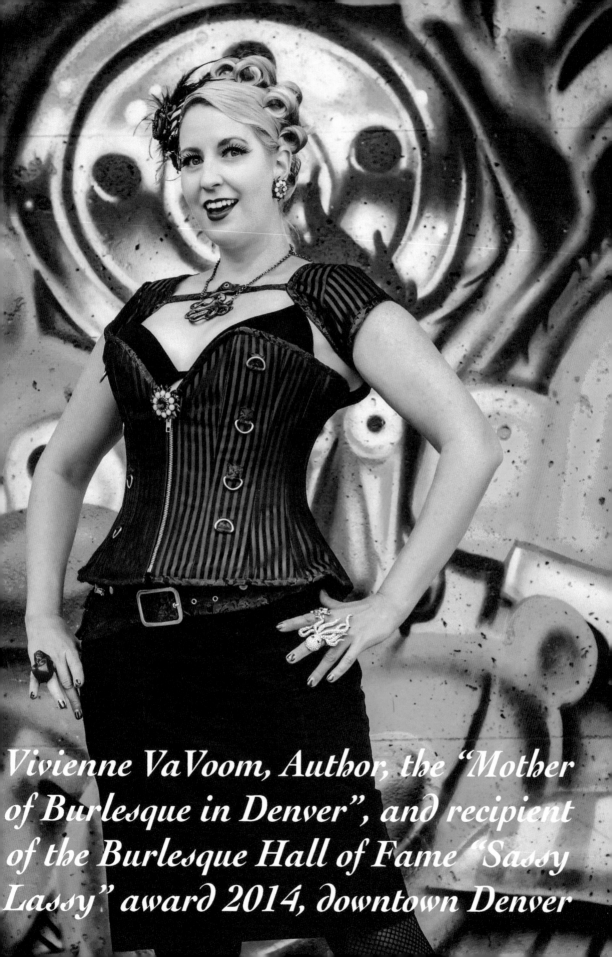

Vivienne VaVoom, Author, the "Mother of Burlesque in Denver", and recipient of the Burlesque Hall of Fame "Sassy Lassy" award 2014, downtown Denver

VAVOOM VELVETY POTATO

This potato soup is a favorite for football Sunday, for some reason. I think it's marvelous anytime!

DIFFICULTY LEVEL:
- Easy

INGREDIENTS:
- 6 bacon strips, diced
- 3 cups cubed peeled potatoes
- 14-1/2 oz chicken broth
- 1 small carrot, grated
- 1/2 cup chopped onion
- 1 tablespoon dried parsley flakes
- 1/2 teaspoon each celery seed, salt and pepper
- 3 tablespoons all-purpose flour
- 3 cups of milk (2% fat is best)
- 8 ounces cheddar/jack cheese cubes
- 2 green onions, thinly sliced

DIRECTIONS:
- In a large saucepan, cook bacon until crisp; drain.
- Add the potatoes, broth, carrot, onion, parsley, celery seed, salt and pepper.
- Cover and simmer until potatoes are tender, about 15 minutes.
- For chunky soup: Combine flour and milk until smooth; add to soup. Bring to a boil; boil and stir for 2 minutes.
- For smooth soup: Cool and then use immersion blender. Add flour/milk mixture and reheat.
- Add cheese; stir until cheese is melted and the soup is heated through. Garnish with green onions.

VARIATIONS:
- Vegetarian: substitute vegetable broth and vegan cheese

 RYAN RECOMMENDS:
"12 Degree Brewing has a brew called Velour Fog that pairs perfectly with this soup. The huge sour flavor and massive ABV keeps you pleasingly tipsy while enjoying this dish."

Rhi Long, at Denver's
Botanic Gardens

RHI-LLY AMAZING WILD MUSHROOM

This is a very fancy soup that is absolute Heaven by the spoonful. It's rich, but light enough to serve at feasts, such as Thanksgiving, without ruining anyone's appetite for turkey, stuffing, gravy, cranberries, mashed potatoes, pie and..oh, my, do I love Thanksgiving!

DIFFICULTY LEVEL:
- Moderate

INGREDIENTS:
- I small handful fresh crimini or portobello mushrooms, chopped
- Olive oil
- 2 ⅔ cps mixed fresh wild mushrooms (e.g. chanterelle, shiitake, porcini, oyster), clean and sliced (reserve some for garnish)
- 2 cloves garlic
- I red onion, minced

- I handful fresh thyme
- salt and pepper
- 4 qts chicken or vegetable stock
- I handful fresh Italian parsley, chopped
- I tablespoon mascarpone cheese (fancy) or sour cream (easy)
- truffle oil, (optional and totally decadent garnish)

DIRECTIONS:
- Heat garlic and oil in soup pot. When you can smell the garlic, remove it from the oil, slice it thinly and set aside. Add the mushrooms, onion, thyme, salt, and pepper. Cook 20 minutes, or until most of the liquid is absorbed.
- Season to taste, add sliced garlic back to the pan -- be careful not to let it burn -- and then stock. Bring to a boil and simmer 20 minutes. Remove half the soup to a deep bowl and

purée with immersion blender, then return to soup pot, adding the parsley and mascarpone or sour cream.
- Serve topped with reserved mushrooms and a drizzle of truffle oil, accompanied by crostini. Absolutely sensational for your dinner parties and a Thanksgiving favorite, chez Frenchie!

VARIATIONS:
- Vegetarian: substitute vegetable stock, vegan cheese

RYAN RECOMMENDS:
"This mushroom soup has an amazing and rather delicate flavor profile; it would be a shame to overwhelm it with an over-the-top brew. Give Blue Ski Lager from Epic Brewing a go; it's an expertly-made lager that's light, crisp and refreshing."

Stacy D. Luxe, at Voodoo Comedy Playhouse

TOMATO D. LUXE

This soup will ruin you for canned tomato soup forevermore. I mean it. You're welcome.

DIFFICULTY LEVEL:

- Easy

INGREDIENTS:

- 3 tablespoons olive oil
- 1 1/2 cups chopped red onions (about 2 onions)
- 2 carrots, peeled and chopped
- 1 tablespoon minced garlic (about 3 cloves)
- 4 pounds roma tomatoes, coarsely chopped (about 5 large)
- 1 1/2 teaspoons sugar

- 1 tablespoon tomato paste
- 1/4 cup chopped fresh basil leaves, plus a few whole basil leaves, for garnish
- 3 cups chicken stock
- 1 tablespoon kosher salt
- 2 teaspoons freshly ground black pepper
- 3/4 cup heavy cream
- Croutons, for garnish

DIRECTIONS:

- Heat the garlic in the olive oil in a large stockpot over medium-low heat. Remove garlic as soon as you can smell the aroma. Chop garlic and set aside.
- Add the onions and carrots and saute for about 10 minutes, until very tender.
- Add the tomatoes, sugar, tomato paste, basil, chicken stock, chopped garlic, salt, and pepper and stir.

- Bring the soup to a boil, lower the heat, and simmer, uncovered, for 30 to 40 minutes, until the tomatoes are very tender.
- Add the cream, remove from heat and cool. Blend with an immersion blender, or in batches in a regular blender. Blend until smooth and discard any pulp/skin.
- Reheat the soup over low heat just until hot and top with basil leaves and/or croutons.

VARIATIONS:

- Vegetarian: use vegetable stock and substitute coconut milk for cream

 RYAN RECOMMENDS:

"There can be only one brew to go with this outstanding tomato soup: Left Hand Brewing's Milk Stout. You won't regret it."

Cora Vette, at the Black Crown Lounge

CLASSIC VETTE BROCCOLI CHEESE SOUP

Forget the smelly, overcooked broccoli soup you've had before. This soup is crazy good!

DIFFICULTY LEVEL:

- Easy

INGREDIENTS:

- 2-3 cups fresh broccoli
- 2 cups chicken broth
- ½ cup white onions, finely diced
- ½ cup baby carrots, finely diced
- 1 clove garlic, minced
- 4 tablespoons unsalted butter
- ⅓ cup all-purpose flour

- ½ teaspoon salt
- ½ teaspoon black pepper
- pinch of paprika
- 1 cup whole milk
- 1 cup heavy whipping cream
- 1½ cup sharp cheddar cheese, shredded
- ½ cup smoked gouda cheese, cubed or shredded

DIRECTIONS:

- Steam, or blanch and shock, broccoli until cooked (do not overcook: broccoli should be firm and bright green).
- Chop cooked broccoli and set aside.
- In a medium stockpot, add chicken broth, onion, carrots and garlic. Bring to a boil and then reduce heat and simmer for 15 minutes or until onions are tender. Set aside.
- In a small saucepan, warm the milk and cream, taking care not to scald.

- In a large pot or deep skillet, melt butter over medium heat. Whisk in flour, stirring constantly for about 1-2 minutes to create a roux. Reduce heat if flour starts to brown. Add in salt, pepper and paprika and continue to stir for 1 minute. Slowly stir in milk and heavy cream, chicken broth mixture, and cheeses.
- Season to taste.
- Top with broccoli pieces and serve to greedy, drooling people at your dinner table.

VARIATIONS:

- Vegetarian: use vegetable broth and substitute coconut milk for cream, use vegan cheese
- Decadence: substitute a really stinky blue or gorgonzola cheese for the cheddar/gouda

 RYAN RECOMMENDS:

"This rich soup fairly requires big flavor from a beer. I give you Dry Dock Brewing Co.'s Double IPA. The sour notes and huge hops are just right for refreshing your palate."

Surlie J. Temple, at 3
Kings Tavern

SWEET AND SURLIE PEA SOUP

So simple and so perfect; no wonder pea soup is so many people's favorite kind!

DIFFICULTY LEVEL:
- Easy

INGREDIENTS:
- 1 large ham hock
- 1 lb peas
- 1 small onion diced
- 1 tbsp chopped garlic

- 1/2 lb (about 6) chopped carrots
- 2 cups of chicken broth
- water (enough to cover)

DIRECTIONS:
- Add all ingredients into the stockpot, add water to cover.
- Cook on low heat until the peas are tender, about 5 hours.

- Remove ham hock and blend with immersion blender to desired consistency.
- If soup is too thick, thin with water or broth.
- Serve with a crisp green salad and garlic olive oil smeared baguette.

VARIATIONS:
- Vegetarian: eliminate ham hock and substitute vegetable broth

 ## RYAN RECOMMENDS:

"This soup cries out for something refreshing — and sassy. Bring Twisted Pine's Cucumber Cream to this party. The cucumber cleans your palate while the medium body reminds you that you are definitely not drinking water."

Midnite Martini, Miss Exotic World 2014, The Reigning Queen of Burlesque, at Lannie's Clocktower Cabaret

MOROCCAN MIDNITE BUTTERNUT BISQUE

Think you don't like squash? Think again, darling. This soup will convert the most stubbornly anti-veg among you, I promise.

Specialty grocery stores will have the Moroccan spices for this recipe but if you can't find them, substitute pumpkin pie spices for Ras el Hanout and substitute chili paste for Harissa.

You can adjust the amount of Harissa to make this soup more or less spicy to suit your taste.

DIFFICULTY LEVEL
- Moderate

INGREDIENTS
- 1 large yellow onion (chopped)
- 1 1/2 tablespoons olive oil
- 2 pounds butternut squash (peeled, seeded, chopped into 1 1/2-inch chunks)
- 2 tablespoons tomato paste
- 1 teaspoon Ras el Hanout (Moroccan spice mix)
- 4 cups hot water
- 1/2 cup heavy cream
- 1/4 pound goat cheese (crumbled)
- 1 teaspoon harissa paste (Middle Eastern chili paste)
- Salt, kosher, of course
- Fresh ground pepper

DIRECTIONS
- Prep the vegetables
- Heat onion, salt and oil in your pot until onions are soft
- Add squash and tightly lid the pot. Steam for about 20 minutes.
- Add spices and water and bring to boil
- Remove from heat and puree (with an immersion blender or in batches using a stand blender)
- Add the cream, goat cheese, tomato paste and the harissa and blend until velvety smooth
- Return to low-to-medium heat, season with salt and pepper
- Pour into bowls (4-6 servings) and top with some goat cheese

 RYAN RECOMMENDS:

"The spice in this soup is hard to overcome — why fight it? Pair with Good Juju, a ginger-infused beer by the folks at Left Hand Brewing. The bite of ginger steps up to the soup without overwhelming it."

RECIPES

Chapter: Beans and Legumes

"Soup puts the heart at ease, calms down the violence of hunger,
eliminates the tension of the day, and awakens and refines the appetite."

Auguste Escoffier

"Beans, beans, the musical fruit..." Beans and legumes are not technically fruit, but I find these recipes do sing! Try the soups in this chapter, and fall in love with these tasty staples all over again.

Dried or fresh beans and pulses, or legumes, are always preferable to canned, when making soup. Even frozen beans and pulses are a better choice than the canned versions, in my opinion. It's really not a big deal to soak the dried versions overnight and my stars does it make a difference in taste and ease of digestion.

Fanny Fitztightlee, at 3 Kings Tavern

OOH LA LA LENTIL

Many of the soups in this chapter require a hambone or other meaty flavor, and, indeed, the vegetarian versions we've tried are sad and dull by comparison. On the other hand, the gentle lentil needs little in the way of embellishment and is a shining example of deliciously simple bean soup that's easily amenable to vegetarian or vegan needs.

DIFFICULTY LEVEL:
- Easy

INGREDIENTS:
- 1 tablespoon olive oil
- 1 medium celery stalk, small dice
- 1 medium carrot, peeled and small dice
- 1/2 medium yellow onion, small dice
- 3 medium garlic cloves, minced
- Kosher salt
- Freshly ground black pepper

- 1 quart vegetable broth
- 15 ozs diced tomatoes with their juices
- 1 1/4 cups lentils (any color except red), rinsed
- 1 bay leaf
- 1/4 teaspoon finely chopped fresh thyme leaves
- 1 teaspoon red wine vinegar or sherry vinegar
- 2 ounces spinach leaves (about 1/2 a bunch)

DIRECTIONS:
- Heat the oil in a large saucepan over medium heat until shimmering, about 3 minutes.
- Add the celery, carrot, and onion and cook, stirring occasionally, until the vegetables have softened, about 10 minutes.
- Stir in the garlic and cook until fragrant, about 1 minute.
- Season with several generous pinches of salt and pepper.
- Add the broth, tomatoes with their juices, lentils, bay leaf, and thyme and stir to combine.

- Cover and bring to a simmer, about 15 minutes.
- Once simmering, reduce the heat to low and continue simmering, covered, until the lentils and vegetables are soft, about 15 minutes more.
- Taste and season with more salt or pepper as needed, then stir in the vinegar.
- Add the spinach and stir until wilted.
- If you prefer a creamier texture, purée half of the soup in a blender and add it back to the pot.

VARIATION:
- Add your favorite kind of sausage and a handful of rice to make this a very fulfilling entrée

RYAN RECOMMENDS:
"Not a beer, but I couldn't resist adding Wild Cider's Hard Apple Cider for this recipe. It's Gluten-free, but don't hold that against it: it's also crisp, refreshing, dry — but sweet enough to stand alongside this delicious soup without overwhelming it."

Chaz Boudoir, in Downtown

HOBO HAM AND BEAN

Although this recipe is ridiculously easy to make (not to mention inexpensive to make), I promise your lucky guests or family will eat like kings.

DIFFICULTY LEVEL:

- Easy

INGREDIENTS:

- 2 pounds dried navy beans
- four quarts hot water
- 1 1/2 pounds smoked ham hocks
- 1 onion, chopped
- 2 tablespoons butter
- salt and pepper to taste

DIRECTIONS:

- Wash the navy beans and run hot water through them until they are slightly whitened.
- Place beans into pot with hot water.
- Add ham hocks, cover, and simmer approximately 3 hours, stirring occasionally.
- Remove ham hocks and set aside to cool.
- Dice meat and return to soup.
- In a small sauté pan, lightly brown the onion in butter. Add to soup.
- Before serving, bring to a boil and season with salt and pepper.
- Accompany with some gorgeous mashed potatoes for a hearty meal.

RYAN RECOMMENDS:

"A soup with navy beans must have rum involved, I say, so go with Great Storm Brewing's Rum Raisin Stout a try. The molasses notes bring that rum flavor and the low ABV means you'll stay vertical in the kitchen long enough to finish making the soup."

Sapphire Stone, at Coors Field

SAPPHIRE'D-UP BEANS AND GREENS

This hearty soup warms and fulfills like nobody's business and makes for a complete meal!

DIFFICULTY LEVEL:
- Easy

INGREDIENTS:
- 1/4 cup olive oil
- 1/2 pound ground sweet Italian sausage
- 2 1/2 cups onion, diced
- 1 teaspoon chili flakes
- 12 cups chicken stock
- 1/2 pound (1 cup) dried navy beans or great northern beans
- 1 bay leaf
- 15.5 oz cannellini beans
- 8 cups collard greens leaves (washed and roughly chopped)
- Grated Pecorino Romano or Parmesan cheese
- Salt and pepper (to taste)

DIRECTIONS:
- Place a soup pot over medium high heat and add the olive oil. When the oil is hot, add the onions with a large pinch of salt. Cook the onions until they start to soften, about 3 minutes.
- Add the sausage, breaking it up into smaller pieces as you add it to the pot. When the sausage starts to brown, add the chili flakes, and cook for another minute.
- Add the chicken stock, dried beans, and bay leaf, and bring the liquid up to a gentle boil.
- After the soup comes up to a boil, reduce it to a simmer and cook for an hour on medium low heat, stirring occasionally.
- After an hour, add the can of cannellini beans with their liquid.
- Cook for another 30 minutes.
- After 30 minutes, add all of the collard greens to the pot with a little more salt and pepper.
- Cook for another 10 minutes.
- To serve, ladle the soup into bowls and top with grated cheese

VARIATIONS:
- Vegetarian/Vegan: omit or substitute with vegan "sausage", use vegetable stock enriched with bouillon, omit or substitute vegan cheese, if desired.

RYAN RECOMMENDS:
"I figure, why try to fight against the big flavors in this soup? Pair with Odell's Mountain Standard Black IPA. The bitterness is the perfect foil for the sweet-spicy-sour-salty taste explosion of this dish. For the sophisticated palate, of course. (Or to expand the one you have.)"

RECIPES

Chapter: Seafood

Seafood soups are the most aromatic and instantly recognizable; you'll never mistake a New England Clam Chowder for anything else, while Paella and Gumbo define their regions like no other food.

Unfortunately, they're among the hardest soups to make and the ingredients are not the cheapest. But it's worth it. You won't regret that little extra time and money when you finally slurp up a bowl of homemade seafood soup, friend.

Neil Dreger and Laura Loredo, at Denver's restored Union Station

HARMONY CLAM CHOWDER

DIFFICULTY LEVEL:
- Easy

INGREDIENTS:
- 6 -7 pieces bacon, cut into small pieces
- 1 medium onion, chopped
- 10 oz. clams, with juice reserved
- 6 -7 potatoes, cubed
- 2 (10 1/2 ounce) Tetra-Pak/cans Cream of Celery soup
- 1 cup heavy cream
- 1 cup milk
- 1 tablespoon butter
- 1 teaspoon dried dill weed

DIRECTIONS:
- Heat bacon until crispy.
- Add onion and cook until translucent.
- Add clam *juice* and potatoes.
- Cook and cover until potatoes are fork tender, about 15-20 minutes, stir occasionally so potatoes won't stick.
- Add clams, soup, cream, milk, and dill weed; add butter and stir
- Cook 30-45 minutes or until thickened, stirring occasionally
- Serve in a warmed crock topped with fresh dill and accompanied by a sourdough roll

RYAN RECOMMENDS:
"It's tempting to throw something with huge flavor at a hearty soup like this; instead I'll suggest Odell's 5 Barrel Ale. It's not overly bitter, overly sweet, or overly sour, it's just a really well-made beer whose crisp hops flavor stand up to the rich creaminess of this soup and leave you wanting more."

Fathom Swanson, The Fastest Tassles in the West, in Deidre von Derriere's kitchen

UNFATHOMABLY GOOD LOBSTER BISQUE

"You can't eat this soup standing up, your knees buckle."

Jerry Seinfeld

DIFFICULTY LEVEL:
- Challenging

INGREDIENTS:
- Lobster claw and tail meat
- 2 tablespoons minced shallots
- 2 tablespoons chopped green onions
- 3 garlic cloves, crushed
- 1/4 cup white wine
- 2 teaspoons Worcestershire sauce
- 2 teaspoons Tabasco sauce
- 1 teaspoon dried thyme

- 6 tablespoons dry sherry
- 1 teaspoon paprika
- 1 cup seafood stock
- 4 ounces tomato paste
- 2 bay leaves
- 2 cups heavy whipping cream
- 4 tablespoons butter

DIRECTIONS:
- In a sauté pan heat oil over medium-high heat and sauté shallots, onions, and garlic for one minute.
- Deglaze the pan with the white wine.
- Add the Worcestershire, tabasco, and thyme and sauté for another minute.
- Deglaze the pan with the sherry.
- Add the paprika, hot water and lobster and combine well.

- Stir in tomato paste and add the bay leaves.
- Simmer 10 minutes.
- Whisk in heavy cream and the butter and bring to a boil.
- Add the lobster and simmer until cooked through.
- Serve with warm, crusty garlic bread.

RYAN RECOMMENDS:
"Upslope's Belgian Style Pale is the perfect beer to accompany this decadent soup. It's dry, sour, and elegant. Taken together with this dish, the two are like that couple at the party everyone is insanely jealous of, yet can't help adoring."

Sarah Taggart, at Denver's historic Paris on the Platte café and bookstore

BOUILLABAISSE (MARSEILLE-STYLE)

"Bouillabaisse, this golden soup, this incomparable golden soup which embodies and concentrates all the aromas of our shores and which permeates, like an ecstasy, the stomachs of astonished gastronomes. Bouillabaisse is one of those classic dishes whose glory has encircled the world, and the miracle consists of this: there are as many bouillabaisses as there are good chefs or cordon bleus. Each brings to his own version his special touch."

Curnonsky (The Prince of Gastronomy)

It's a favorite memory. An ancient great-aunt in a flowery dress and apron, standing outside her house near Grasse in the South of France, stirring an enormous vat of Bouillabaisse and swearing at anyone who dared come near. She sang to the pot as she cooked.

DIFFICULTY LEVEL:
- Challenging

INGREDIENTS:
- 2 large onions, chopped
- 1/2 cup olive oil, divided
- 4 tomatoes, chopped
- 1 large bouquet garni (fresh herbs tied together, such as parsley, rosemary, thyme, tarragon, basil, whatever you like)
- 4 cloves garlic, crushed
- 1 large strip orange zest
- 1 teaspoon saffron threads
- 1 1/2 pound potatoes, cubed
- 12 pounds assorted fresh fish, cleaned and prepared (classic choices: conger, scorpion fish, sea bass, whiting, monkfish, octopus, crab, spiny lobster, angler fish)
- Salt and pepper
- Baguette, sliced and toasted

DIRECTIONS:
- In a large stockpot set over medium-low heat, cook the onions in 1/4 cup of the olive oil until they turn translucent and tender.
- Add the chopped tomatoes, bouquet garni, garlic, orange zest, saffron, and potatoes to the pot.
- Generously season the vegetables with salt and pepper.
- Layer the prepared seafood over the vegetables.
- Drizzle the seafood with the remaining olive oil and allow it to rest for a minimum of 10 minutes.
- Pour just enough hot water over the vegetables and seafood to cover all the ingredients.
- Bring the stew to a full boil for 15 minutes.
- Place the toasted baguette slices in the bottom of soup bowls and ladle the bouillabaisse over the bread.
- Faint with joy.

RYAN RECOMMENDS:
"Well, gallons of French table wine, of course. Failing that, I'd go with Great Storm Brewing's Sine on Oaked Golden Strong. It'll put up a good fight. Light, fruity notes don't try to compete with the perfection of the soup, while adding a fun flavor dimension."

Gigi D'Lovely, at Voodoo
Comedy Playhouse

D'LOVELY GUMBO

My friends, many of whom are featured in the photos of this book, held a fundraiser so I could self-publish this book. As thanks, I served this gumbo to the hordes who came to hear live music and take in a burlesque show.

It is now a thing of legend.

You can do this, and you'll be glad you did. Also, it freezes unbelievably well! Tradition holds you use a cast iron cauldron for this and I do believe, mes chers, it adds to the whole Voodoo ambiance of this soup/stew.

Now, you certainly can find and use frozen or canned seafood in this, and utilize ready-made fish stock, but I recommend that you make it to the letter at least once, to get the experience (and bragging rights).

DIFFICULTY LEVEL:
- Crazy Challenging

INGREDIENTS:
- 5 quarts water
- I dozen fresh crabs, raw, boiled or steamed – have seafood counter clean them!
- 2 pounds medium to large shrimp, peeled and deveined (reserve the shells and heads to make seafood stock)
- 2 lbs smoked sausage, such as chorizo or kielbasa, cut into 1" rounds (1 lb each of two different sausages is optimal)
- 3/4 pound andouille sausage, cut into 1 inch rounds
- 2 pounds okra, cut into rounds
- 1/2 cup plus 2 tablespoons vegetable oil
- 1/2 cup all-purpose flour

- 2 large onions, coarsely chopped
- 6 large cloves garlic, chopped
- I bunch flat-leaf parsley, chopped
- 5 stalks celery, chopped
- I bunch green onions, tops and bottoms, chopped
- I large green bell pepper, chopped
- I pound crab meat, picked and cleaned of shells and cartilage
- 2 tablespoons Creole seasoning
- 4 bay leaves
- 4 tablespoons filé powder
- Salt and pepper to taste
- 6 cups steamed white rice

DIRECTIONS:
- If you haven't had the seafood counter clerk clean the crabs, do this first (it's a dirty job!) Clean the crabs, removing the lungs, heart and glands and other parts so that only the pieces of shell containing meat (including the legs, swimmers and claws) remain. Refrigerate the meaty parts of the crabs.
- Put the portions of the crabs that have been removed into a 6- or 8-quart stockpot. Add the shrimp heads and shells and 5 quarts water to the pot and bring to a boil over high

heat. Reduce the heat to low and simmer for 30 minutes. Remove from the heat.
- Cook the sausages in a skillet in batches over medium heat, turning occasionally, until the pieces are slightly brown and much of the fat has been rendered. Remove the sausage and set aside on a paper towel-lined plate to drain. Discard the excess fat remaining in the skillet before cooking the next batch of sausage.
- Once all the sausage has been cooked, wipe the excess oil from the skillet, being careful

not to scrub away those bits of sausage that have stuck to the bottom of the skillet.

- Add the 2 tablespoons vegetable oil. Heat the oil over medium heat and then add the okra. Lower the heat to medium and cook the okra until it is slightly brown and dried, stirring frequently, about 45 minutes.

- ROUX: While the okra cooks, place the 1/2 cup vegetable oil in a 12-quart stockpot. Heat the oil over medium heat. Once the oil is hot, one tablespoon at a time slowly add the 1/2 cup flour to prepare the roux, stirring constantly. Once all the flour has been added, continue heating and stirring the roux until it becomes a medium brown color, somewhere between the color of caramel and milk chocolate, about 10-15 minutes.

- Add the onions to the roux, stirring constantly. Once the onions are wilted, add the garlic, parsley, celery, green onions and bell pepper.

- Strain the seafood stock into the large stockpot. Add the browned sausage and bay leaves and bring everything to a boil over medium-high heat. Then reduce the heat to medium and continue to cook.

- Once the okra is cooked, add it to the gumbo pot. Continue cooking the gumbo for 60 minutes.

- Add the reserved crabs and shrimp and cook for 15 minutes longer. Remove the gumbo from the heat and stir in the Creole seasoning and filé powder. Let the gumbo rest for 15 to 20 minutes. As it cools, oil should form on the top. Skim the oil with a ladle or large spoon and discard. Stir in the picked crab meat. Taste the gumbo and adjust seasoning with more salt and pepper as needed. Serve the gumbo ladled over steamed rice.

Then drink 5-6 Hurricanes and congratulate yourself on succeeding in this Herculean task. I suggest setting out sturdy bowls and spoons and selling it to passerby at a premium. The scent alone will drive any Louisiana-bred hungry person for 50 miles directly to your door.

RYAN RECOMMENDS:

"Well, this being a New Orleans staple, I imagine you'd want to drink a Hurricane or 5. If I may suggest an alternative that's less dangerous? Nearly any beer goes well with this gumbo, but I recommend Hop Vivant's Imperial IPA by Mountain Sun. Big hops flavor and a light sourness gives it strength to withstand the awesomeness of gumbo. This is a tremendous pairing for game day, in particular, though not if you are invested at all in the game."

RECIPES

Chapter: Cold Soups

"I live on good soup, not on fine words."

Moliere

Cherry Pop Pop Poppins,
in downtown Denver

POP-POP POPPIN' GAZPACHO

Summer soups are pure bliss. Liquid magic. Of all the gorgeous, fresh, delicious summer (cold) soup recipes I considered, none capture this magic better than these two soups, you potentially could source right from your garden. Pair with a salad and a glass of wine or Sangria and you've got yourself the Most Perfect Summer Meal.

DIFFICULTY LEVEL:
- Easy

INGREDIENTS:
- 3 lb. ripe tomatoes, peeled, seeded, coarsely chopped
- 2 slices of white bread, crust removed
- 2 cucumbers, peeled, seeded, coarsely chopped
- 1 small red onion, coarsely chopped
- 3 cloves of garlic, minced
- 2 green bell peppers (or any sweet green pepper)

- 6 tablespoons extra virgin olive oil
- 3 tablespoons red wine vinegar
- Salt and pepper
- Garnish: 1 tsp each of cucumber and green pepper, finely chopped
- Optional extra garnish: 3-4 croutons

DIRECTIONS:
- Soak the bread in a small amount (few tablespoons) of water. Gently remove and squeeze dry.
- Place the tomatoes, bread, cucumbers, onions, garlic and peppers in a blender or food processor -- you may have to blend in batches, depending on the size of your blender or processor.

- Blend until the mixture is smooth and pour into a large non-metallic bowl.
- Stir in the oil and vinegar.
- Add salt and pepper to taste.
- Mix well, cover and refrigerate for at least 1 hour.
- Garnish with the chopped vegetables and croutons, if desired.
- Serve gazpacho chilled.

VARIATIONS:
- Substitute coconut milk or soy yogurt for sour cream

RYAN RECOMMENDS:
"A refreshing soup like this calls for its boozy equal and Odell's Double Pilsner fills that role wonderfully. It's lightly sour and deliciously crisp, making it a perfect pairing for a hot summer day."

Chakra T. Ease, at her Yoga studio

CHAKRA TEASIN' CHILLED CUCUMBER AVOCADO (A RAW VEGAN RECIPE)

Raw vegan food really comes into its own in the summertime, with readily-available fruits and vegetables. Embrace it.

This easy-to-make soup is rapturously good and so fresh, it's like vitamin soup. If you can keep it chilled, this is amazing for a picnic lunch.

DIFFICULTY LEVEL:

- Easy

INGREDIENTS:

- 1 lb. cucumbers, roughly chopped
- 2 avocados, cut into small pieces
- ¼ cup fresh lime juice (about 2 limes)
- ¾ cup water
- Salt and pepper
- Garnish: chopped tomato and cilantro

DIRECTIONS:

- Place the cucumbers, avocados, lime juice, water, sea salt, and pepper into a blender.
- Process ingredients until smooth.
- Season to taste.
- Transfer the soup to a large bowl or storage container and chill in the fridge for at least an hour before serving.
- Garnish with fresh, chopped tomato and cilantro.

RYAN RECOMMENDS:

"A vegan soup requires a vegan beer. Luckily, Colorado offers many of those and for this dish I'd highly recommend Colorado Kind from Mountain Sun. A hoppy, amber beer, it's beautifully refreshing. Promise you'll love it!"

PHOTOGRAPHERS

Mark Palmer is a professional photographer based in Denver, Colorado. He specializes in entertainment event photography and business and social networking portraiture. He also enjoys being a part of the burlesque community by capturing the shows and backstage hijinks.

Email him at mark@palmerpics.com or find him on the Web at www.PalmerPics.com.

www.PALMERPICS.com
MARK PALMER PHOTOGRAPHY

www.palmerpics.com

mark@palmerpics.com

850-274-1555

Dave - Dirty D Photography

I can't remember a time when I didn't find myself drawn to photography. I started shooting as a casual hobby about 15 years ago, but didn't dive into it until about 7 years ago. What continues to fuel my passion for photography is how a single image can make you laugh till you're stomach hurts or rip your heart out of your chest. Photography can capture not just the real physical joy and sadness of life, it can also express ideas and feelings that sometimes words cannot. I find myself drawn to the stark yet subtle emotion that can be captured by black and white photography, so that is what I would say I specialize in and am most passionate about. Since I began taking photos, my experiences have covered: sports, performance, events, promotional, product, portraiture, bands/music, nature, landscape, abstract/experimental…. basically I just want to capture moments and feeling and share them with people… some good, some bad, but all real.

Ant Graham - Broken Glass Photography

"A mini-bio? Oh dear God. Okay, let's try this. I am 45 years old. I have a wife, a son, a bunny and a cat that I spend much of my time adoring and arguing with (often at the same time). I live in Colorado Springs, CO (where we try art, but mostly we just build more churches). I'm an award winning professional photographer who makes very little money, so I am truly at one with the artistic universe."

CONTRIBUTORS

Ryan Hodros has dreamt of being a professional writer since the age of five, and of being a professional drinker since 21. He's been writing about beer since January of 2014, about China since 2008, and about whatever fictional stories he could dream up since 1987. Having grown up in a small town in Northeast Ohio, he earned a BA in English and religious studies from Baldwin-Wallace College in Berea, Ohio in 2005. Ryan left the Heart of It All in 2006 for the tender embrace of the US Navy, where he met Tressa Medley, who would make the mistake of marrying him in 2010. A sailor-turned-culinary-professional, she's currently a pastry chef in downtown Denver.

Stationed at Pearl Harbor, Ryan transformed Mandarin Chinese and into English for Uncle Sam for over four years before getting an AA in Mandarin from the Defense Language Institute and Foreign Language Center. Upon his triumphant return to the Mainland, Ryan attended the Auguste Escoffier School in Boulder, CO, getting an education in both the Pastry and Culinary Arts. It's there he met the unstoppable Frenchie Renard, which is how his recommendations wound up in the book you're currently reading.

Ryan considers himself something of a professional adventurer, having a resume so diverse, it's hard to say exactly what he's done the most. He's been a janitor, camp counselor, climbing wall belayer, nature guide, literary magazine selection staff member, event organizer, YMCA staff manager, editor, cell phone customer care rep, construction worker, translator, sailor (though he's never seen the inside of a Navy ship), desk jockey, clueless computer analyst, struggling author, beer reviewer, copy editor, and fact checker. He's trained in everything from CPR to camp songs.

With a laissez-faire philosophy when it comes to beer and beer pairing, Ryan's sums up his thoughts thusly: "The best beer is one you enjoy, and anyone who tries to give you a hard time about it is a snob that you should humor, but ignore. Don't feel like there's only one beer for whatever meal you're currently eating, and if you pick the wrong one, we 'experts' are going to laugh at you. Beer is a beverage of inclusion and friendliness, and true beer guys and gals only give recommendations to help you to enjoy yourself. So make sure you do!"

A versatile vixen of the classic ecdysiasts art, Vivienne VaVoom can generally be found bumping and grinding a mile high in her hometown of Denver. Known for her "Timeless Tease" style, this classic co-quette has performed around the country and the world, including Miss Exotic World, Tease-O-Rama, New York Burlesque Fest, the Helsinki Burlesque Fest and Miss Burlesque New Zealand. Vivienne is dedicated to increasing the population of burlesque queens in Denver with her monthly School of Burlesque lessons. In 2013 she celebrates 15 years on the burlesque stage. Her alter ego, Michelle Baldwin, wrote THE book on the neo-burlesque scene, *Burlesque and the New Bump & Grind.*

ABOUT THE AUTHOR

A French kid who grew up in suburban Denver, Colorado, Alex McCall, a/k/a Frenchie Renard's, youth was spent watching '70's sitcoms and learning to cook for her mom and three sisters. Luckily, PBS cooking shows and her mom's pile of French cookbooks were on hand with step-by-step instruction, and Mom adored throwing dinner parties once she figured out the free, live-in catering bit.

An avid reader and total dance nerd, Frenchie dreamed of one day being a Solid Gold Dancer who wrote best-selling novels on the side. A problematic boy-craziness, combined with wanderlust and copious alcohol, derailed this grand plan and she ended up back in Denver with a trail of published articles, a dented and damaged body, and five feral children.

Enter Burlesque, a glamorous, hilarious, magical and often misunderstood world of sequins, glitter, dance, and incredibly talented people who share her love of dance and slapstick comedy. She found her spiritual home there among the sparklefolk.

Interestingly, it eventually became very clear that Frenchie was just too jazzy for the kind of corporate work in which she'd found herself, and soon left it behind to pursue her life's passion and a more nourishing career in culinary arts. She enrolled at the prestigious Auguste Escoffier School of Culinary Arts, moved the family compound to Boulder, Colorado, and set about becoming an embarrassment to her children and a rather long-in-the-tooth line cook. This is Frenchie Renard's first cookbook, you are hereby warned it will not be the last.

Made in the USA
Charleston, SC
08 January 2015